Applied Psychology

Volume 2

MAKING YOUR OWN WORLD

Being the Second of a Series of Twelve Volumes on the Applications of Psychology to the Problems of Personal and Business Efficiency

BY

WARREN HILTON, A.B., L.L.B.

FOUNDER OF THE SOCIETY OF APPLIED PSYCHOLOGY

ISSUED UNDER THE AUSPICES OF

THE LITERARY DIGEST.

FOR

The Society of Applied Psychology

NEW YORK AND LONDON

1920

1914

BY THE APPLIED PSYCHOLOGY PRES

SAN FRANCISCO

Republished from the public domain by

Creative English Publishing

www.Creative-English-Institute.com

Under Classic Reads

August 2013

**ISBN-13:
978-1492139089**

**ISBN-10:
1492139084**

CONTENTS

Chapter I
THE TWO FUNDAMENTAL PROCESSES OF MIND,
P11

MIND AS A MEANS TO ACHIEVEMENT

THREE POSTULATES FOR THIS COURSE

EXPERIENCE AND ABSTRACTIONS

PRIMARY MENTAL OPERATIONS

Chapter II
SENSATIONS AND OUR PERCEPTION OF THEM,
P15

MIND'S SOURCE OF SUPPLIES

DOES MATTER EXIST?

FIRST-HAND KNOWLEDGE

SECOND-HAND KNOWLEDGE

ETHERIC VIBRATIONS AS CAUSING

SENSATIONS

THE ROAD TO PERCEPTION

THE PLACE WHERE SENSATION OCCURS

LABORATORY PROOF OF SENSE-PERCEPTIVE PROCESS

REACTION-TIME

THE HUMAN TELEPHONE

THE LIVING TELEGRAPH

THE SIX STEPS TO REACTION

UNOPENED MENTAL MAIL

SELECTIVE PROCESS THAT DETERMINES CONDUCT

IN TUNE WITH LIFE-INTEREST

PRACTICAL ASPECTS OF PERCEPTION PROCESS

Chapter III
SENSORY ILLUSIONS AND SUGGESTIONS FOR THEIR USE, P33

UNRELIABILITY OF SENSE-ORGANS

BEING AND SEEMING

USE OF ILLUSIONS IN BUSINESS

MAKING AN ARTICLE LOOK BIG

TESTING THE CONFIDENTIAL MAN

TESTS FOR CREDULITY

WHAT COLORS LOOK NEAREST

TESTING THE RANGE OF ATTENTION

A GUIDE TO OCCUPATIONAL SELECTION

TEST FOR ATTENTION TO DETAILS

OTHER BUSINESS APPLICATIONS

Chapter IV
INWARDNESS OF ENVIRONMEN, P47

FACTORS OF SUCCESS OR FAILURE

SHOULD SEEING BE BELIEVING?

HEARING THE LIGHTNING

IMPORTANCE OF THE MENTAL MAKE-UP

UNREALITY OF "THE REAL"

"THINGS" AND THEIR MENTAL DUPLICATES

EFFECT OF CLOSING ONE'S EYES

IF MATTER WERE ANNIHILATED

IF MIND WERE ANNIHILATED

AS MANY WORLDS AS MINDS

Chapter V
ESSENTIAL LAW OF PRACTICAL SELF-MASTERY,
P59

OPTION AND OPPORTUNITY

PRE-ARRANGING YOUR CONSCIOUSNESS

HOW TO DEFINITELY SELECT ITS ELEMENTS

AN INFALLIBLE RECIPE FOR SELF-POSSESSION

USING "UNSEEN EAR PROTECTORS"

HOW TO AVOID WORRY, MELANCHOLY

PUTTING CIRCUMSTANCES UNDER FOOT

RUNNING YOUR MENTAL FACTORY

ACQUIRING MENTAL BALANCE

DISSIPATING MENTAL SPECTERS

HOW TO CONTROL YOUR DESTINY

Chapter I

THE TWO FUNDAMENTAL PROCESSES OF MIND

Mind as a Means to Achievement

In the preceding book, "Psychology and Achievement," we established the truth of two propositions:

I. All human achievement comes about through bodily activity.

II. All bodily activity is caused, controlled and directed by the mind.

To these two fundamental propositions we now append a third, which needs no proof, but follows as a natural and logical conclusion from the other two:

III. The Mind is the instrument you must employ for the accomplishment of any purpose.

Three Postulates for this Course

With these three fundamental propositions as postulates, it will be the end and aim of this Course of Reading to develop plain, simple and specific methods and directions for the most efficient use of the mind in the attainment of practical ends.

To comprehend these mental methods and to make use of them in business affairs you must thoroughly understand the two fundamental processes of the mind.

These two fundamental processes are the Sense-Perceptive Process and the Judicial Process.

The Sense-Perceptive Process is the process by which knowledge is acquired through the senses. Knowledge is the result of experience and all human experience is made up of sense-perceptions.

Experience and Abstractions

The Judicial Process is the reasoning and reflective process. It is the purely "intellectual" type of mental operation. It deals wholly in abstractions. Abstractions are constructed out of past experiences.

Consequently, the Sense-Perceptive Process furnishes the raw material, sense-perceptions or experience, for the machinery of the Judicial Process to work with.

Primary Mental Operations

In this book we shall give you a clear idea of the Sense-Perceptive Process and show you some of the ways in which an understanding of this process will be useful to you in everyday affairs. The succeeding book will explain the Judicial Process.

Chapter II

SENSATIONS AND OUR PERCEPTION OF THEM

Mind's Source of Supplies

Whatever you know or think you know, of the external world comes to you through some one of your five primary senses, sight, hearing, touch, taste and smell, or some one of the secondary senses, such as the muscular sense and the sense of heat and cold.

The impressions you receive in this way may be true or they may be false. They may constitute absolute knowledge or they may be merely mistaken impressions. Yet, such as they are, they constitute all the information you have or can have concerning the world about you.

Does Matter Exist?

Philosophers have been wrangling for some thousands of years as to whether we have any real and absolute knowledge, as to whether matter actually does or does not exist, as to the reliability or unreliability of the impressions we receive through the senses. But there is one thing that all scientific men are agreed upon, and that is that such knowledge as we do possess comes to us by way of perception through the organs of sense.

If you have never given much thought to this subject, you have naturally assumed that you have direct knowledge of all the material things that you seem to perceive about you. It has never occurred to you that there are intervening physical agencies that you ought to take into account.

First-Hand Knowledge

When you look up at the clock, you instinctively feel that there is nothing interposed between it and your mind that is conscious of it. You seem to feel that your mind reaches out and envelops it.

As a matter of fact, your sense impression of that bit of furniture must filter through a great number of intervening physical agencies before you can become conscious of it.

Direct perception of an outside reality is impossible.

Second-Hand Knowledge

Before you can become aware of any object there must first arise between it and your mind a chain of countless distinct physical events.

Modern science tells us that light is due to undulations or wave-like vibrations of the ether, sound to those of the air, etc. These vibrations are transmitted from one particle of ether or air to another, and so from the thing perceived to the body of man.

Think, then, what crisscross of air currents and confusion of ether vibrations, what myriad of physical events, must intervene between any distant object and your own body before sensations come and bring a consciousness of that object's existence!

Nor can you be sure, even after any particular vibration has reached the surface of your body, that it will reach your mind unaltered and intact!

Etheric Vibrations as Causing Sensations

What goes on in the body itself is made clear by your knowledge of the cellular structure of man.

You know that you have a system of nerves centering in the brain and with countless ramifications throughout the structural tissues of the body.

You know that part of these nerves are sensory nerves and part of them are motor nerves. You know that the sensory nerves convey to the brain the impressions received from the outer world and that the motor nerves relay this information to the rest of the body coupled with commands for appropriate muscular action.

DIAGRAM

SHOWING THE FOUR CHIEF ASSOCIATION CENTERS OF THE HUMAN BRAIN DIAGRAM SHOWING THE FOUR CHIEF ASSOCIATION CENTERS OF THE HUMAN BRAIN

The Road to Perception

The outer end of every sensory nerve exposes a sensitive bit of gray matter. These sensitive, impression-receiving ends constitute together what is called the "sensorium" of the body.

When vibrations of light or sound impinge upon the sensorium, they are relayed from nerve cell to nerve cell until they reach the central brain. Then it is, and not until then, that sensations and perceptions occur.

Consider, now, the infinitesimal size of a nerve cell and you will have some conception of the number of hands through which the message must pass before it is received by the central office.

Many of our sensations, especially those of touch, seem to occur on the periphery of the body—that is to say, at that part of the exposed surface of the body which is apparently affected. If your finger is crushed in a door, the sensation of the blow and the pain all seem to occur in the finger itself.

The Place Where Sensation Occurs

As a matter of fact, this is not the case, for if one of your arms should be amputated, you would still feel a tingling in the fingers of the amputated arm. Thus has arisen a superstition that leads many people to bury any part of the body lost in this way, thinking that they will never be entirely relieved of pain until the absent member is finally at rest.

Of course, the fact is that you would only seem to have feeling in the amputated arm. The sensation would really occur in the central brain tissue as the organ of the governing intelligence, the organ of consciousness.

Laboratory Proof of Sense-Perceptive Process

And you may set it down as an established principle that all states of consciousness, whether seemingly localized on the surface of the body or not, are connected with the brain as the dominant center.

The facts we have been recounting have been established by the experiments of physiological psychology. Thus, the work of the laboratory has shown that between the moment when a sense vibration reaches the body and the moment when sensation occurs a measurable interval of time intervenes.

If your eyes were to be blindfolded and your hand unexpectedly pricked with a white-hot needle, the time that would elapse before you could jerk your hand away could be readily measured in fractions of a second with appropriate instruments.

Reaction Time

This interval is known as reaction-time. It varies greatly with different persons. During this reaction-time, the cell or cells attacked upon the surface of the hand have conveyed news of the assault through numberless intermediate sensory nerve cells to the brain. The brain in turn has sent out its mandate through the appropriate motor nerve cells to all the muscle and other cells surrounding the injured cell, commanding them to remove it from the point of danger.

The work of the nervous system in dealing with the ether vibrations that are constantly impinging upon the surface of the body has been likened to that of the transmitter, connecting wire and receiver of a telephone. Air-waves striking against the transmitter of the telephone awaken a similar vibratory movement in the transmitter itself. This movement is passed along the wire to the receiver, which vibrates responsively and imparts a corresponding wave-like motion to the air.

The Human Telephone

These air-waves when heard are what we call sound.

In the same way, air-waves striking the ear are communicated by the auditory nerve to the brain, where they awaken a corresponding sensation of sound. But these waves must be vibrating at between 30 and 20,000 times a second. If they are vibrating so slowly or so rapidly as not to come within this range, we cannot hear them.

The Living Telegraph

This process is by no means a mechanical affair. On the contrary, it is a series of mental acts. Every cell in the living telegraph must receive the message and transmit it. Every cell must exercise a form of intelligence, from the auditory cell reporting a sound-wave or the skin cell reporting an injury to the muscle cells that ultimately receive and understand a message directing them to remove the part from danger.

Reaction-time, so called, is thus occupied by cellular action in the form of mental processes intervening between the nerve-ends and the brain center, in much the same way that light and sound vibrations intervene between the object perceived and the surface of the body.

The Six Steps to Reaction

For even the simplest of sense-perceptions we have, then, this sequence of events: first, the object perceived; second, the series of vibrations of ether particles intervening between the object and the body; third, the impression upon the surface of the body; fourth, the series of mental processes, cell after cell, in the nerve filaments leading to the brain; fifth, when these impressions or messages have reached the brain, a determination of what is to be done; and, sixth, a transmission by cellular action of a new message that will awaken some response in the muscular tissues.

Unopened Mental Mail

This process is completely carried out, however, in only comparatively few instances. The vast majority of sense-impressions awaken no reaction. They are registered in the mind, but they are not perceived. We are not conscious of them. They form a part, not of consciousness, but of sub consciousness. They are messages that reach the mind but are laid aside like unopened mail because they possess no present interest.

Wherever and however you may be placed, you are always and everywhere immersed in a flood of etheric vibrations. Light, sound and tactual vibrations press upon you from every side. At a busy corner of a city street these vibrations rise to a tumultuous fortissimo; in the hush of a night upon the plains they sink to pianissimo. Yet at every moment of your day or night they are there in greater or less degree, titillating the unsleeping nerve-ends of the sensorium.

Selective Process
that Determines Conduct

Your mind cannot take time to make all these sense-impressions the subject of conscious thought. It can trouble itself only with those that bear in some way upon your interests in life.

Your mind is like the receiving apparatus of the wireless telegraph which picks from the air those particular vibrations to which it is attuned. Your mind is selective. It is discriminating. It seizes upon those few sensory images that are related to your interests in life and thrusts them forward to be consciously perceived and acted upon. All others it diverts into a subconscious reservoir of temporary oblivion.

In Tune with Life-Interest

You will have a clearer understanding of the sense-perceptive processes and a more vital realization of the practical significance of these facts when you consider how they affect your knowledge of material things and your conception of the external world.

This subject possesses two distinct aspects.

One aspect has to do with the inability of the sense-organs to record the facts of the outer world with perfect precision. These organs are the result of untold ages of evolution, and, generally speaking, have become wonderfully efficient, but they display surprising inaccuracies. These inaccuracies are called Sensory Illusions.

Practical Aspects
of Perception Process

The other aspect of the Sense-Perceptive Process has to do with the mental interpretation of environment.

Both these aspects are distinctly practical.

You should know something of the weaknesses and deficiencies of the sense-perceptive organs, because all your efforts at influencing other men are directed at their organs of sense.

You should understand the relationship between your mind and your environment, since they are the two principal factors in your working life.

Chapter III

SENSORY ILLUSIONS AND SUGGESTIONS FOR THEIR USE

Unreliability of Sense-Organs

Figure 1 shows two lines of equal length, yet the vertical line will to most persons seem longer than the horizontal one.

Figure 1.

In Figure 2 the lines A and B are of the same length, yet the lower seems much longer.

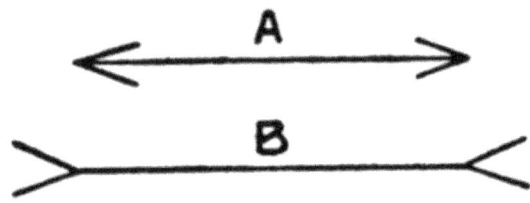

Figure 2.

Those things look smallest over which the eye moves with least resistance.

In Figure 3, the distance from A to B looks longer than the distance from B to C because of the time we involuntarily take to notice each dot, yet the distances are equal.

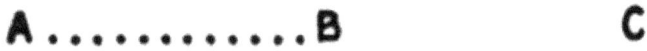

Figure 3.

Being and Seeming

For the same reason, the hatchet line (A–B) appears longer than the unbroken line (C–D) in Figure 4, and the lines E and F appear longer than the space (G) between them, although all are of equal length.

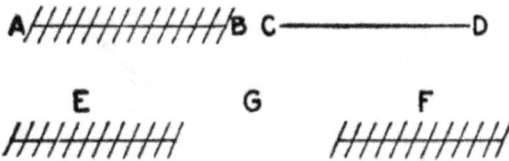

Figure 4.

Filled spaces look larger than empty ones because the eye unconsciously stops to look over the different parts of the filled area, and we base our estimate upon the extent of the eye movements necessary to take in the whole field. Thus the filled square in Figure 5 looks larger than the empty one, though they are of equal size.

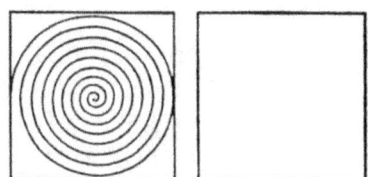

Figure 5.

White objects appear much larger than black ones. A white square looks larger than a black one. It is said that cattle buyers who are sometimes compelled to guess at the weight of animals have learned to discount their estimate on white animals and increase it on black ones to make allowances for the optical illusion.

THIS BOY ARE OF EQUAL HEIGHT, BUT ASSOCIATION OF IDEAS MAKES THE MAN LOOK MUCH THE LARGER THIS MAN AND THIS BOY ARE OF EQUAL HEIGHT, BUT ASSOCIATION OF IDEAS MAKES THE MAN LOOK MUCH THE LARGER

Use of Illusions in Business

The dressmaker and tailor are careful not to array stout persons in checks and plaids, but try to convey an impression of sylph-like slenderness through the use of vertical lines. On the other hand, you have doubtless noticed in recent years the checkerboard and plaid-covered boxes used by certain manufacturers of food products and others to make their packages look larger than they really are.

The advertiser who understands sensory illusions gives an impression of bigness to the picture of an article by the artful use of lines and contrasting figures. If his advertisement shows a picture of a building to which he wishes to give the impression of bigness, he adds contrasting figures such as those of tiny men and women so that the unknown may be measured by the known. If he shows a picture of a cigar, he places the cigar vertically, because he knows that it will look longer that way than if placed horizontally.

Making an Article Look Big

A subtle method of conveying an idea of bigness is by placing numbers on odd-shaped cards or blocks, or on any blank white space. The object or space containing the figures always appears larger than the corresponding space without the figures.

This fact has been made the basis of a psychological experiment to determine the extent to which a subject's judgment is influenced by suggestion. To perform this experiment cut bits of pasteboard into pairs of squares, circles, stars and octagons and write numbers of two figures each, say 25, 50, 34, 87, etc., upon the different pieces. Tell the subject to be tested to pick out the forms that are largest. The susceptible person who is not trained to discriminate closely will pick out of each pair the card that has the largest number upon it.

Testing the Confidential Man

This test can be made one of a series used in examining applicants for commercial positions. It can also be used to discover the weakness of certain employees, such as buyers, secretaries and others who are entrusted with secrets and commissions requiring discretion, and who must be proof against the deceptions practiced by salesmen, promoters and others with seductive propositions.

Tests for Credulity

This examination can be carried still further to test the subject's credulity or power of discrimination. What is known as the "force card" test was originally devised by a magician, but has been adopted in experimental psychology. Take a pack of cards and shuffle them loosely in the two hands, making some one card, say the ace of spades, especially prominent. The subject is told to "take a card." The suggestive influence of the proffered card will cause nine persons out of ten to pick out that particular card.

Turning from illusions of suggestion, shape and size, another field of peculiar sensory illusions is found in color aberration. Some colors look closer than others. For instance, paint an object red and it seems nearer than it would if painted green.

What Colors Look Nearest

Aside from the obvious uses to which these sense-illusions can be put, they form the basis for a number of psychological experiments to test the abilities of persons in many ways. Here is a test which deals with the range of attention. If you desire to discover the capacity of any person to pay attention to unfamiliar questions or subjects which might at some future time have great importance, try this test. Have a piece of pasteboard cut into squares, circles, triangles, half-moons, stars and other forms. Then write upon each piece some such word as hat, coat, ball or bat. The objects are then placed under a cloth cover and the subject to be examined is told to concentrate his attention on the shapes alone, paying no attention to the words. The cloth is lifted for five seconds and then replaced. The subject is then told to draw with a pencil the different shapes and such words as he may chance to remember. The experiment should then be repeated, with the injunction to pay no attention to the shapes but to remember as many words as possible, and write them down on such forms as he may happen to recall.

Testing the Range of Attention

Of course, the real object is to determine whether the subject will see more than he is told, or whether he is a mere automaton. The result will tell whether his attention is of the narrow or broad type. If it be narrow, he will see only the forms in the first case and no words, and in the second case he will remember the words but be unable to recall the shape of the pieces of cardboard.

A Guide to Occupational Selection

His breadth of attention will be shown by the number of correct forms and words combined which he is able to remember in both cases. In other words, this will measure his ability to pay attention to more than one thing at a time.

Other things being equal, the narrow type of attention belongs to a man fitted for work as a bookkeeper or mechanic, while the broad type of attention fits one for work as a foreman or superintendent or, lacking executive ability, for work requiring the supervision of mechanical operations widely separated in space.

Test for Attention to Details

The ordinary man sees but one thing at a time, while the exceptional man sees many things at every glance and is prepared to remember and act upon them in emergency.

Having determined a person's scope of attention, you may want to test his accuracy in details as compared with other men. To conduct such an experiment dictate a statement which will form one typewritten letterhead sheet. This statement should comprise facts and figures about your business of which the subjects to be tested are supposed to have accurate knowledge. After this original page is written, have your typist write out another set of sheets in which there are a large number of errors both in spelling and figures. Then have each of the persons to be examined go through one of these sheets and cross out all the wrong letters or figures. Time this operation. The man who does it in the quickest time and overlooks the fewest errors, naturally ranks highest in speed and accuracy of work.

Other Business Applications

Look into your own business and you will undoubtedly find some department, whether it be store decoration, office furnishing, window dressing, advertising, landscape work or architecture, in which a systematic application of a knowledge of sensory illusions will produce good results.

Chapter IV

INWARDNESS OF ENVIRONMENT

Factors of Success or Failure

The aspect of the sense-perceptive process that deals with the relation of mind to environment is of greatest practical value.

Look at this subject for a moment and you will see that the world in which you live and work is a world of your own making. All the factors of success or failure are factors of your own choosing and creation.

If there is anything in the world you feel sure of, it is that you can depend upon the "evidence of your own senses," eyes, ears, nose, etc. You rest serene in the conviction that your senses picture the world to you exactly as it is. It is a common saying that "Seeing is believing."

Should Seeing Be Believing?

Yet how can you be sure that any object in the external world is actually what your sense-perceptions report it to be?

You have learned that a countless number of physical agencies must intervene before your mind can receive an impression or message through any of the senses.

Under these conditions you cannot be sure that your impression of a green lamp-shade, for instance, comes through the same sort of etheric and cellular activities that convey a picture of the same lamp-shade to the brain of another. If the physical agencies through which your sense-impressions of the lamp-shade filter are not identical with the agencies through which they pass to the other person's brain, then your mental picture and his mental picture cannot be the same. You can never be sure that what both you and another may describe as green may not create an entirely different impression in your mind from the impression it creates in his.

Other facts add to your uncertainty. Thus, the same stimulus acting on different organs of sense will produce different sensations. A blow upon the eye will cause you to "see stars"; a similar blow upon the ear will cause you to hear an explosive sound. In other words, the vibratory effect of a touch on eye or ear is the same as that of light or sound vibrations.

Hearing the Lightning

The notion you may form of any object in the outer world depends solely upon what part of your brain happens to be connected with that particular nerve-end that receives an impression from the object.

You see the sun without being able to hear it because the only nerve-ends tuned to vibrate in harmony with the ether-waves set in action by the sun are nerve-ends that are connected with the brain center devoted to sight. "If," says Professor James, "we could splice the outer extremities of our optic nerves to our ears, and those of our auditory nerves to our eyes, we should hear the lightning and see the thunder, see the symphony and hear the conductor's movements."

Importance of the Mental Make-Up

In other words, the kind of impressions we receive from the world about us, the sort of mental pictures we form concerning it, in fact the character of the outer world, the nature of the environment in which our lives are cast—all these things depend for each one of us simply upon how he happens to be put together, simply upon his individual mental make-up.

There is another way of examining into the intervening agencies that influence our mental conception of the material world about us.

Unreality of "The Real"

Look at the table or any other familiar object in the room in which you are sitting. Has it ever occurred to you that this object may have no existence apart from your mental impression of it? Have you ever realized that no object ever has been or ever could be known to exist unless there was an individual mind present to note its existence?

If you have never given much thought to questions of this kind, you will be tempted to answer boldly that the table is obviously a reality, that you have a direct intuitive knowledge of it, and that you can at once assure yourself of its existence by looking at it or touching it. You will conceive your perception of the table as a sort of projection of your mind comfortably enfolding the table within itself.

"Things" and their Mental Duplicates

But perception is obviously only a state of mind. Can it, then, go outside of the mind to meet the table or even "hover in midair like a bridge between the two"? If you perceive the table, must not your perception of it exist wholly within your own mind? If, then, the table has any existence outside of and apart from your perception of it, then the table and your mental image of the table are two separate and distinct things.

In other words, you are on the horns of a dilemma. If you insist that the table exists outside of your mind, you must admit that your knowledge of it is not direct, immediate and intuitive, but indirect and representative, because of intervening physical agencies, and that the only thing directly known is the mental impression of the table. On the other hand, if you insist that your knowledge of the table is direct, immediate and intuitive you must admit that the table is only a mental image, a mental reality, if it is any sort of reality at all, and that it has no existence outside of the mind.

Effect of Closing One's Eyes

You may easily convince yourself that the table you directly perceive can be nothing other than a mental picture. How? Simply close your eyes. It has now ceased to exist. What has ceased to exist? The external table of wood and glue and bolts? By no means. Simply its mental duplicate. And by alternately opening and closing your eyes, you can successively create and destroy this mental duplicate.

If Matter Were Annihilated

Clearly, then, the table of which you are directly and immediately conscious when your eyes are open is always this mental duplicate, this aggregate of color, form, size and touch impressions; while the real table, the physical table, may be something other than the one of which you are directly aware. This other thing, this physical table, whatever it is, can never be directly known, if indeed it has any existence, a fact that many distinguished philosophers have had the courage to deny.

Imagine, then, for a moment that everything except mind should suddenly cease to exist, but that your sense-perceptions—that is to say, your perception of sensory impressions—were to continue to follow one another as before. Would not the physical world be for you just exactly what it is today, and would you not have the same reasons for believing in its existence that you now have?

If Mind Were Annihilated

And, conversely, if the world of matter were to go on, but all mental images, all perception of sense-impressions, were to come to an end, would not all matter be annihilated for you when your perceptions ceased?

It is obvious that the world is not the same for all of us; but that it is for each one of us simply the world of his individual perceptions.

As Many Worlds as Minds

The whole subject of sense-impressions, sensation and perception may, therefore, be looked at from the standpoint of the mind as an active influence, as well as from the standpoint of outside objects as the exciting causes of sense-impressions.

Chapter V

ESSENTIAL LAW OF PRACTICAL SELF-MASTERY

Option and Opportunity

External objects excite sensory impressions, but the perception of them is purely at the option of the mind.

This is of the greatest practical importance. Consider its consequences. It means that sense-impressions and your perception of them are two very different things. It means that sense-impressions may throng in upon you as they will. They are the work of external stimuli impressing themselves upon the sensorium as upon a mechanical register. You are helpless to discriminate among them. You cannot accept some and exclude others. You are a perambulating dry plate upon which outside objects produce their images.

Prearranging Your Consciousness

But, and this is a vital distinction, perception is an act of the mind. It is initiated from within. It permits you to discriminate among sensations in the sense that you may dwell upon some and ignore others. It enables you to definitely select, if you will, the elements that shall make up the content of your consciousness.

Perception as an independent mental process thus enables you to predetermine what elements of passing sensory experience may be made the basis of your conscious judgments and of your feelings and emotions.

How to Definitely Select its Elements

Bear this in mind when you think of your environment and its supposed influence upon your life. Remember that your environment is no hard-and-fast thing, an aggregate of physical realities. Your environment, so far as it affects your judgment and your conduct, is made up, not of physical realities, but of mental pictures.

Your environment is within you. Get this conclusion clearly in your mind.

Hold fast to the point of view that, Environment, the environment that influences your conduct and your life, is not a chance massing of outward circumstances, but is the product of your own mind.

An Infallible Recipe for Self-Possession

Think what this means to you. It means that by deliberately selecting for attention only those sense-impressions, those elements of consciousness, that can serve your purpose, you can free yourself from all distractions and make peaceful progress in the midst of turmoil.

Using "Unseen Ear Protectors"

"In the busiest part of New York, a broker occupied a desk in a room with six other men who had many visitors constantly moving about and talking. The gentleman was at first so sensitive to disturbances that he accomplished almost nothing during business hours, and returned home every evening with a severe headache. One day a man of impressive personality and extremely calm demeanor entered the office, and noticing the agitated broker, smilingly said: 'I see that you are disturbed by the noise made by your neighbors in the conduct of their affairs; pardon me if I leave with you an infallible recipe for peace in the midst of commotion: Hear only what you will to hear.' With this terse counsel he quietly bade the astonished listener adieu. After his visitor had departed, the nervous man felt unaccountably calm, and was constrained to meditate upon his friend's advice, and no sooner did he seek to put it into practical use than he learned for the first time that it was his rightful prerogative to use unseen ear protectors as well as to employ his ears. Six or seven weeks elapsed before he saw his mysterious visitor again, and by that time he had so successfully practiced the simple though forceful injunction, that he had reached a point in self-control where the Babel of tongues about him no longer reached his consciousness."

How to Avoid Worry, Melancholy

Herein lies a remedy for worry, with its sleepless nights and kindred torments; for melancholy and despair, with their train of physical and financial disaster.

How? Simply by shutting off the flow of disagreeable thoughts and substituting others that are pleasant and refreshing.

You are master. You can change the setting of your mental stage from portentous gloom to sunlit assurance. You can concentrate your thought upon the useful, the helpful and the cheerful, ignore the useless and annoying, and make your life a life of hope and joy, of promise and fulfillment.

Putting Circumstances Under Foot

You will not question the statement that what you do with your life is the combined result of heredity and environment. At the same time you doubtless possess a more or less hazy belief in the freedom of your own will.

The chances are that in any previous reflections on this subject you have magnified the influence of outside agencies and wondered just how a man could make himself the master rather than the victim of circumstances.

You now realize that your environment is an environment of thought, that your material universe is a thing your own making, and that you can mold it as you will simply by the intelligent control of your own thinking.

Running Your Mental Factory

In Book I. you learned that—

I. All human achievement comes about through bodily activity.

II. All bodily activity is caused, controlled and directed by the mind.

In this volume you have added to these propositions a third, namely:

III. The mind is the instrument you must employ for the accomplishment of any purpose.

Acting on this third postulate, you have begun the consideration of primary mental operations with a view to evolving methods and devices for the scientific and systematic employment of the mind in the attainment of success. You have concluded your study of the first of the two fundamental processes of the mind, the Sense-Perceptive Process, and have learned to distinguish between seeing or hearing or feeling on the one hand and perceiving on the other.

Acquiring Mental Balance

Realizing this distinction and applying it to your daily life, you can at once set to work to acquire mental poise and practical self-mastery, the essence of personal efficiency.

There never has been a moment in all your life when sense-impressions were not pouring in upon you from every side, tending to disturb and annoy you and interfere with your concentration and progress. Heretofore you have struggled blindly with these distracting influences, not knowing the elements with which you had to deal nor how to deal with them.

Dissipating Mental Specters

But the mask has been torn from the specter of distraction, and hereafter when irrelevant sights, sounds and other sensations threaten to interrupt your work, just stop a moment and consider. So far as you and your actual knowledge are concerned, nothing exists in substance and reality outside your mental picture of it. So far as you and your actual knowledge are concerned, all matter is simply thought, and you have never doubted your ability to dismiss a thought. It is for you, then, here and now, to decide whether you will harbor sensory pictures that impede your progress and allow them to harass and dominate you and interfere with the achievement of your ambition, or whether you will ignore these intruders and thereby annihilate them.

How to Control Your Destiny

Success is a variable term. In the last analysis, it means simply getting the thing that you want to have.

Whether you succeed or fail depends altogether upon your own attitude toward the external facts of life.

You have within you a living Force against which all the world is powerless. You have only to know it and to learn how to use it.

Learn the lesson of your own powers, the secret of controlling the selective and creative energy within you, and you can bring any project to the goal of accomplishment.

In the closing volumes of this Course we shall instruct you in practical methods by which the selection of those elements of experience that are helpful may be made absolutely automatic.

Applied Psychology

Volume 1: Psychology and Achievement

Volume 2: Making your own World

Volume 3: Driving Power of Thought

Volume 4: The Trained Memory

Volume 5: Power of Mental Imagery

Volume 6: Psychic Energy

Volume 7: Processes and Personality

Volume 8: Mind Mechanism

Volume 9: Mind Mastery

Volume 10: Technique of Success

Volume 11: External Efficiency Factors

Volume 12: Specific Applications

www.ingramcontent.com/pod-product-compliance
Lightning Source LLC
Chambersburg PA
CBHW071623170526
45166CB00003B/1174